Mealtime
Blessings

40 Prayers to Sing and Say

Church Health Center
Memphis, TN

About the Church Health Center
The Church Health Center seeks to reclaim the church's biblical commitment to care for our bodies and our spirits. Long recognized as a national model for serving the uninsured, the Center has spent years connecting people of faith and their congregations with quality health resources and educational experiences. To learn more about the Center, visit ChurchHealthCenter.org. To learn more about our magazine on health ministry, *Church Health Reader*, visit chreader.org.

Mealtime Blessings: 40 Prayers to Sing and Say © 2012 Church Health Center, Inc. Memphis, TN

Second Printing, 2013

ISBN: 978-1-62144-030-7

Printed in the United States of America

Prayers by Kira Dault and the Church Health Center's Child Life Education and Movement staff.

Design and layout by Lizy Heard.

The Church Health Center welcomes your feedback. Please send your comments to FCO@churchhealthcenter.org.

Introduction

About *Mealtime Blessings*

Mealtime Blessings brings child-friendly rhymes and themes to your family's table. These 40 prayers grow out of years of success in the Child Life Education and Movement area of the Church Health Center. Through daily programming, Child Life helps children receive healthy food as a gift from God.

How to Use *Mealtime Blessings*

Young children enjoy the cadence of rhymes and simple songs. The sung prayers use familiar tunes. For children, mastering the repetition both grows their sense of confidence and reinforces the meaning of the words they say. For adults, the prayers are simple reminders of deeper truths. Consider these ideas for making praying the blessing a family affair.

- Say the prayers in short phrases and ask children to repeat.
- Once a child has mastered the blessing, let the child lead the family in prayer.
- As you begin to eat, repeat phrases and talk about what they mean.
- Invite your child to make up simple movements to go with the words.
- Keep simple supplies handy and create art with your child to illustrate key concepts or words.

As you ask God to bless your meals with your children, we pray that you find nourishment for both body and spirit.

Blessings to Sing

Song List

 Row, Row, Row Your Boat

 Mary Had a Little Lamb

 Twinkle, Twinkle, Little Star

 Frère Jacques / Are You Sleeping?

 London Bridge Is Falling Down

 The Farmer in the Dell

(To the Tune of Row, Row, Row Your Boat)

Fruits and vegetables,
They're so good for me.
Thank you, God, for healthy food,
My carrots and my peas.

(To the tune of Frère Jacques / Are You Sleeping?)

Healthy food, healthy food
Is good to eat, good to eat.
Thank you for this food.
Thank you for this day.
God is good. God is good.

(To the tune of Mary Had a Little Lamb)

Healthy food is good to eat,
Good to eat, good to eat.
Healthy food is good to eat.
Thank you, God. Amen.

(To the tune of Twinkle, Twinkle Little Star)

Now we eat our healthy food.
Thank you, God, for you are good.
Help my body grow and grow.
Help my mind to learn and know.
Now we eat our healthy food.
Thank you, God, for you are good.

(To the tune of Mary Had a Little Lamb)

In my work and in my play,
In my play, in my play.
Help me to grow strong, I pray.
God, I love you so.

(To the tune of Twinkle, Twinkle Little Star)

Thank you for the birds that sing.
Thank you, God, for everything.
Thanks for legs to run and run.
And for eyes to see the sun.
Thank you for the birds that sing.
Thank you, God, for everything.

(To the tune of Frère Jacques / Are You Sleeping?)

Count your blessings,
Count your blessing.
For the day, for the day.
Healthy food and sunshine.
Music, books and play time.
Thank you, God. Thank you, God.

(To the tune of London Bridge Is Falling Down)

Bring the baskets!
Loaves and fish! Loaves and fish!
Loaves and fish!
Everyone will have a dish!
Bring the baskets!

(To the tune of The Farmer in the Dell)

We thank you for our heart.
We thank you for our heart.
Healthy foods are good to eat.
They take care of our heart.

(To the tune of Twinkle, Twinkle Little Star)

Every time we take a seat,
We thank God for all we eat.
Breakfast, lunch and dinner, too,
For all we eat we will thank you.
Every time we take a seat,
We thank God for all we eat.

(To the tune of Frère Jacques / Are You Sleeping?)

Make me thankful, make me thankful.
God, today. God, today.
Make me strong in body.
Make me strong in spirit.
Now and always. Now and always.

(To the tune of London Bridge Is Falling Down)

Be my guide in all I do,
All I do, all I do.
Playing and eating too,
God, be with me.

(To the tune of The Farmer in the Dell)

God blesses us today!
God blesses us today!
Thank you, God, for healthy food.
God blesses us today!

(To the tune of Mary Had a Little Lamb)

Lord, we praise you all day long,
All day long, all day long.
Lord, we praise you all day long,
And thank you for our food.

(To the tune of Twinkle, Twinkle Little Star)

Thank you, God, for sleep and rest,
And for things I love the best.
Playtime, books, and Mommy, too.
Yummy food to help me grow.
Thank you, God, for sleep and rest,
And for things I love the best.

(To the Tune of London Bridge Is Falling Down)

Thank you for this food today,
Food today, food today.
Food to help me grow and play.
Thank you, God.

(To the tune of Frère Jacques / Are You Sleeping?)

God, our Maker; God, our Maker,
Once again; once again,
We bow our head to thank you.
We bow our head to thank you.
Amen, Amen.

Blessings to Say

Thank you, God, for rain and sun.
Thank you for my legs to run.
Thank you for good food to eat.
Thank you for water, oh so sweet.
Help my body grow so tall.
Help my spirit love one and all.
Amen.

For the needy, God is able.
Bring the hungry to our table.
Teach us not to push and shove.
Teach us how to share God's love.
Amen.

As we sit down to our meal,
Let us take a moment to kneel.
Thank God for fingers and toes,
For my mouth and for my nose.
Thank you, God, for I am blessed
It is God I love the best.
Amen.

Now we pause for daily bread,
Join our hands and bow our heads.
Thanks for what the farmers bring.
Thank you, God, for everything.
Amen.

Apples are red.
Spinach is green.
Eating healthy food
Helps us stay strong and lean.
God gives us food to help us grow
So let's thank our God,
From our head to our toes.
Amen.

I thank God for my fingers,
I thank God for my toes.
I thank God for knees and legs,
I thank God for my nose.
I thank God for this table,
And thank God for this food.
I thank God for everything.
Thank God, for God is good!
Amen.

I like to eat and I like to pray.
So to God today I pray,
Thank you, God, for healthy food.
You, my God, are just and good.
Amen.

Breathe in, breathe out.
Breathe in, breathe out.
God gives us air,
Which we don't think about.
God's hidden gifts are everywhere,
In water and sun and food and air.
Amen.

God loves everyone, even our foes
From the tops of our heads
To our tiniest toes
Because God loves us, God provides
To give us healthy
And wholesome lives.
Thank you, God.
Amen.

God loves my feet that help me stand.
God loves my legs and arms and hands.
God loves my fingers and my toes.
God loves my eyes and ears and nose.
God has made me whole and strong.
So I thank, God, all day long!
Amen.

In the spring, we plant some seeds
And wait for plants to grow—
Not weeds!
When summer comes, we pick the crop,
Tomatoes and lettuce and beans—
The lot!
Autumn is the harvest time—
Pumpkins and wheat for bread and pie.
Winter is the time for rest
With soup and stew and cocoa—
The best!
God gives seasons
And the food they bring,
Thank you, God for everything!
Amen.

We look at this food
As we gather at the table.
And we give thanks to God
For God makes us able
To grow and live such healthy lives.
Thank you, God, for you provide!
Amen.

God is gracious.
God provides
Manna for the Israelites.
God is loving.
God will give
Food to us so we can live.
Amen.

Okra, carrots, squash and peas.
God made the Earth to give us these
And put the balance fair and square
Commanding us to give Earth care.
Amen.

The smallest to the biggest,
God's loving care for all
Is daily bread we all require.
Young and old, short or tall.
Amen.

We labor through the planting,
And patiently we wait.
We labor through the harvest,
For food to fill our plate.
And now we bow our heads,
For God is good, and God is great!
Amen.

On the long walk to Emmaeus,
Though they'd heard what Jesus said,
Their eyes were truly opened
With the breaking of the bread.
Amen.

Broccoli, carrots, and zucchini, too.
Vegetables are good for you.
Green, red, and yellow,
They make us strong.
They give us strength to play and play
All day long.
Thank you, God.
Amen.

Stomp your feet!
Clap your hands!
Let's give thanks to God and dance!
God gives us life!
God gives us food!
God fills our table,
Because God is good!
Amen.

Asparagus, zucchini, and rutabaga, too.
These are plants that are good for you.
They are also words that are fun to say,
So let's have fun with vegetables today!
Thank you, God.
Amen.

I look around and all I see
Has been provided for you and me.
God gives us food and air
And everything because God cares.
So let us pause and bow our heads
And give thanks to God
For our daily bread.
Amen.

Here is my body. Here is my spirit.
God, please take care of me today.
Help me to grow.
Help me to love you more.
This I pray.
Amen.

The hungry here are welcome
For God is love of all
And bids us share the bounty
Across dividing walls.
Amen.

Your Mealtime Blessings

Use this space to record some of your favorite mealtime blessings.

Alphabet Appetite: Teaching Children Healthy Eating through the Alphabet is a faith-based, healthy living curriculum for children ages 2-5 years. It is designed to be used in churches, classrooms and other community groups as a way to introduce children to healthy foods. Each lesson also builds literacy and fine motor skills, increases vocabulary and enhances cognition and development.

Find this resource online at
www.ChurchHealthCenter.org/Store

Rethink the separation of church and health.